My Father's Drawer

poems by

Jennie Mintz

Finishing Line Press
Georgetown, Kentucky

My Father's Drawer

Copyright © 2021 by Jennie Mintz
ISBN 978-1-64662-488-1 First Edition
All rights reserved under International and Pan-American Copyright Conventions. No part of this book may be reproduced in any manner whatsoever without written permission from the publisher, except in the case of brief quotations embodied in critical articles and reviews.

ACKNOWLEDGMENTS

These poems, or versions of these poems, first appeared in the following journals:

The Comstock Review: "My Father's Drawer"
Harbinger Asylum: "Fugue"
Jewish Literary Journal: "My Jewish Grandmother"
Paterson Literary Review: "Little Dresses"

Publisher: Leah Huete de Maines
Editor: Christen Kincaid
Cover Art: Jane Mintz
Author Photo: Jennie Mintz
Cover Design: Elizabeth Maines McCleavy

Order online: www.finishinglinepress.com
also available on amazon.com

Author inquiries and mail orders:
Finishing Line Press
PO Box 1626
Georgetown, Kentucky 40324
USA

Table of Contents

My Father's Drawer 1

The Face in the Shroud 2

Photograph from Childhood 4

My Jewish Grandmother 5

My Grandmother's Rose Clock 8

Little Dresses 9

My Father in the Mirror 11

A Fire in the Blood 12

Fugue 13

The Mood Swings Still with Me 14

My Father Who Failed as a Savior 15

Photograph of Lanai Pineapple Plantation, 1939 17

The Dutch Windmill Vase 18

Carving Pumpkins, circa 1984 19

Another Tower of Babel 20

For My Japanese Grandfather, An Elegy 21

My Mother is Like the Snowball Flower 23

Playing Old Records in Khartoum 24

Hawaiian Geese 25

For my parents

Steven Paul Mintz
and
Jane Matsue Mintz

My Father's Drawer

In the wooden crooks of his dresser drawers
I find tokens my dead father left behind
like collected seashells.
They speak traces of his thoughts
the way the ocean can whirr, then pause,
such a stone-locked man, a statue so grave
he could stand like Stalin, only to be toppled
and smashed into bits.
But now, I seek him in every corner,
like dust on a spider's web, a fish fleeing
into its own shadow, a darting of the sun's light,
from leaf edge to rippling bark.
At the back of the lower cubby,
cotton handkerchiefs shine like white mushrooms
in the tea-bag dark of its crevices.
There, they bloom like edelweiss,
that sacred flower. The cold touch of foreign coins
glinting from the bottom of a well.
And then, the smell of worldly power,
pink and violet paper currency,
unknown kings and queens from pauper nations.
Yet in the upper drawer, off track, and warped—
I find the little notes I left on his pillow
in a child's scrawl, decorated with cupcakes and fat cats,
the picture frame I made for Mother
and later removed from the wall.
All this he kept, even cherished, or felt too guilty to
throw away, along with his revelation that
the daughter he tried to touch eluded him.
Now I am back, my grown self in a put-away seashell,
buried there in the smallest compartment,
where he laid down his things for reasons
I can only guess, whether to keep from mislaying—
or being sent into time. Not now. Not ever.
My father, lost gold, a voice nothing can hold.

The Face in the Shroud

There is a black and white photograph
of my dead father's face. Passport-like,
in a frame, on his old dark-wooden dresser.

I wonder what my father was thinking
when the camera flashed.
And, I have stared into the grain.
There, images form inside patterns of oak,
the way the image of a face
is seen on the shroud of Jesus.

Some worshipers believe
they found the visage of their savior
within the blood stains on a linen cloth.

Some believe the face of the corpse
should be covered in death,
no gloating at an open grave.
Perhaps, I should have laid my baby cloth
over my father's face, not placed
in the coffin by his side.

Sometimes I think I found a resemblance
of my father in the wood,
as if he was watching over me,
as if he would stay.

After I viewed his body,
I sat in an armchair,
and felt my heart levitate,
a kind of resurrection.
But I knew his ghost
wouldn't rise again
in three days. Only later,
at his memorial service,
did my voice scrape
like a belt-buckle against flesh.

And I remember how I trembled,

my soft-spoken father was shaking me,
as if we still wrestled
even after all these years,
all this human history
pulling us apart.

Photograph from Childhood

Wearing a summer dress,
she sits in a low wicker chair.
The day is warm, the sun a blur of white.

I wear red lace-up shoes
and stand between my mother's legs,
leaning back, elbows resting on the thighs.
From there, I seem to reign.

Years of naïve innocence lie ahead,
gentle as the tropical grass.
A shadow of caves in my mother's lap,
a fossil of love buried there.

My Jewish Grandmother

The menstrual darkness
of bootlegger Blackberry wine
in the glass portico bottle,
was your mother's sleeping pill.
You forged your own escape route
by taking the Xanax,
passing it around, to us,
like a box of imported pecans.

Your parents had sailed
to Ellis Island, leaving behind
the Habsburg Empire,
the shattered storefronts of pogroms,
nights of broken glass,
hiding places, a ghetto armband.

Your Orthodox father
went to temple twice a day
on the lower-east side.
With no need for Talmud scholars, here,
he labored as a garment presser
with the spit hiss of steam,
turning his skin pink as a shank of beef,
snapping on his suspenders,
bringing home a stained bib shirt
to wash and hang dry.

By day, you cried slumped in a chair
in your dark kitchen,
with your bleeding ulcers,
for which you drank warm milk.
You had no use for psychiatric pills.
Craziness, you said, will brand
you from cradle to grave.
You were right.

In Queens, my father walked
on the other side of the street
in his haberdashery suit,
to distance himself from you
with your orange pea coat
over rumpled flower finery.
You sprayed your neighbor
with the garden hose,
and feared reprisal,
triple locking your door.

You slopped together brisket
and liver, elbowing us out of the way,
your bossy whistle-blowing
and *let me do it* battle song.

What pleasure was this?
I loved your smell of mothballs
covered in sweet perfume,
in your paisley housedress,
your pendulous breasts.
When your mood tilted
the blue wobbles in your eye,
cold as the Ukraine sky
your parents left.
Your blue underwear
you grew tired of washing.

When Grandpa died,
you swayed with a bellow,
propped between the pillars
of your two sons,
as they rocked you towards
the deflated old man in his casket—
an accountant, then taxi driver,
owner of a commissary stand
famous for its cotton candy.

Once a week you set your
freckled beef-chunk arms,
swollen from fibromyalgia,
on your vinyl tablecloth,
to your humming task
of filling your checkerboard pillbox.
After the death of your son,
you started taking Paxil,
that you claimed saved your life,
and served us bialy bagels.
You tucked your dentures
into a pink box every night
and mumbled *I love you* to me
like a baby with no teeth.

Now your mouth is like a warm grave.
No more sharp alligator teeth
to bite away emptiness with.
No more glass shards
sparkling in your eyes like blue diamonds.
No more six pointed stars
to scrape away our tainted genes
or chain to darkness.

My Grandmother's Rose Clock

After she died, we inherited it
and hung it from a nail
in the hall, where it still ticks,
the painted numbers and hands
in black calligraphy.
Fatal roses adorn the glass rim
which is calm as the moon,
each one like the lipstick stain
she left on her tissues,
and in the lower-left corner,
between the 6 and 9,
there is an old birdcage
with a still swing inside,
and that silver bird—about to fly
like the dove after the flood
beating its wings, an olive leaf
clutched in its beak, and sealed
into the end of time.

Little Dresses

My Japanese grandmother and her sisters
were gifted in domestic handicraft.
One made our Christmas stockings,
sewing on velvet decorations
and sequins to spell our names.
Another crocheted rainbow soft afghans
that drape over the backs of sofas,
a third assembled Japanese dolls
that sit in a glass case in our living room.

The eggshell doll:
made with bony-fingered arthritic hands.
What it takes to pin open a hole in an egg,
allow the yolk and insides to drain out,
and paint a face on the delicate white.
Such opal elegance rests on a kimono body
with bristles of black horse hair.

The fisherman doll:
this one is *hapa haole*.
He wears a blue kimono with a straw skirt,
knees bent holding a fishing pole,
real hair pulled back in a samurai ponytail;
each strand of hair implanted
one at a time on the plastic skull.

The red kimono doll:
forever leaning slightly forward,
as if meeting you for the first time,
perched on wooden platform sandals.

Yes, my grandmother made little dresses
that rest on built-in white hangers.
Each dress its own print, floral or geometric pattern,
with an apron flap and tied bow in front.
The baby dresses are not made to be worn,
but to store odds and ends within the deep pocket it forms;
the bottom of the dress all sewn together.

I stored them in my closet and on the doorknobs.
I kept pantyhose in one, a wooden back-scratcher
poked out of another.

For years I have watched the patterns change
their shades of blue,
soothing me like the ruffled ocean.
Another dress is a floral print on green
with a cantaloupe orange apron,
this one reminds me of a garden pool.
What hopes she had for me.

Such pretty little dresses.
On the lapel of one is a gold-framed pin that says
she who plants thorns will never gather roses.
I don't remember if it was my mother, or myself,
that picked out that pin.

I was a dying rose, blooming thorns in madness.
I kept a brown bottle of vanilla extract
in my underwear drawer,
but the perfume I wore to school was Poison.

My Father in the Mirror

Dear dead Father,
why do you settle in my bones
like snow seeping into earth,
or a cake pan filled with batter?

A terrified mouse still makes
house in my heart,
sweeping the dust of chimneys.
Alas, those petals always
wander back in spring.
Spring is when you venture out,
breaking out of the body cast
of winter stillness.

Now I see you in my reflection.
The way I brush my teeth is you,
bored, pacing like a musical tune.
The way I can't follow a recipe,
the way I fidget with my forefinger
when lost in anxious thought.

I am your carbon copy,
a smudge of your ink.

Who does the looking glass reveal?
Who is this man's body I may follow?
Whose thoughts did mine take over,
as you tag-team me on your way

to death. Oh Father, to get you out
I could never break enough mirrors,
still asking, no, commanding:
who, who, who?

A Fire in the Blood

The ancients described it
as a fire in the blood, as if
demon or angel slipped into
the flesh, casting its long shadow.

A cryptic language
that is yet to be deciphered.

Fire consumes as it blazes and blisters.
If this is a mountain,
there is a wildfire on one side,
and an oracle on the other
speaking in two different tongues.

How many years will go by clearing
the brush covered by snow cliffs,
the river carrying driftwood and ice floes?

I can only ask myself this:
melancholy: a sudden stillness
that can stop the heart.

Fugue

Little nothings cut out like paper dolls,
each one, identical
and slowly lit on fire,
a chariot without a rider,

falsehood without a truth

a chain of them spinning

into space, then sucked in
and into a black-hole abyss

swallowing another spoonful of stars.

The Mood Swings Still with Me

You were steam coming out
of Mother's teapot,
or an Old Faithful geyser
going off in Yellowstone Park,

the humility of a genie
let out of Aladdin's lamp.

As I grew older, you found
your way between the covers
of my beat up novellas,
each page dog-eared or smudged
with a thumb print.

But now, decades later,
you still come and go like the clashing
of that gold cymbal
high in the sky before sunset,

or the last shadow that shoved you
back in the dark.

My Father Who Failed as a Savior

You were drawn to the smell of cheap
upholstery, and your own sweat.
For our sake, you tried
to bring home roomier cars
but had to accept the hand me downs,
the cars that convulsed, and died
surely as people do from neglect.
That Dodge that broke down
in the middle of the road
to other drivers' hurling insults.

I remember it was the gas
running out, which left us stranded
on the highway in North Carolina.
Where were we going, then, Father?
A family vacation?
You hiked to the nearest exit
in search of a gas station
while my sister and I smoked
our Kool cigarettes,
and sat in the long weeds,
blowing out smoke rings
as we paced the gravel
grinding in our souls—

Don't smoke!
Our grandfather, in the back seat, yelled.

You kept trying to show us
deserts in the American landscape,
tourist traps selling black pottery
from Navajos, or old cowboys
panning for gold, at two dollars an hour
inching our way along the map
into the boondocks of California.

Then there was the canoe trip
we tried down the Shenandoah River,
stuck in the same boat
with no middle person for balance.
We tipped over a few times,
as junk floated downstream
and it started to pour.

We capsized again, you and me,
in the middle of the river,
we went belly up.
Others passed us, smiling and fidgeting
in their life preservers,
orange as prison garb.
Is everything alright?
You smiled, but I knew this was a sentence
without parole.

To capsize is to turn over,
each wobble of our canoe
was like my mind flipped over.
You tried to right it again,
but it never worked, not then or now
and just stayed still.

As you tried to steady
what had already sunk.

Dear Father,
dead more than ten years
under a cloud of earth,
no more than a piddling
of your crossword bones,
how many times did I need to be baptized
in that river, with you,
to know that I loved you,
just as you tried to be my Jewish Khristos,
as if you were the messiah,
as if it would take another
two thousand years just to save me.

Photograph of Lanai Pineapple Plantation, 1939

My young grandmother stands
with the other girls, her sly smirk
suggests she has a sweetheart.

I gaze closer at her face,
her dark eyes lit on the horizon,
sensing the coming of war,
a straw hat, bandages cover her arms—
hazards of unregulated labor.

One of her brothers,
later killed in a factory accident,
looks on.

Just beyond the picture frame,
black and white crops fan out

with more prickly fruit to gather.

The Dutch Windmill Vase

On my desk,
is a small vase from Holland
that my father brought home—
from his travels overseas,
hexagon with six sides,
with a few skittish cracks
running down the rim,
and rather than feeding it
asphodels in bloom,
I leave its mouth empty.

At one time, windmills
were used to send signals
depending on the position
of their blades, someone would
set them at intervals
to convey an event—
such as a wedding or funeral.

Maybe I grew up similarly mute,
arms hoisting up their sails,
refusing to talk to my father,
and the pen I choose now to write his elegy
drawn from the same vase,
my sword, drawn from the earth
where garlands lay.

Carving Pumpkins, circa 1984

A week before Halloween
we drove out to the patch
among scarecrows, corn stalks,
and hay piled in wooden carts,

where the Amish wife
clad in a long prim-fitting dress
and juvenile bonnet, set out
pumpkins on the ground
selling them two for one.

Back home, we scooped out
the orange flesh from the rind
to make jack o'lanterns,
their ghoulish faces, cut out eyes
and crooked mouths,
lit from within with a candle.

Thinking back now, I wonder if
I hadn't swallowed some seeds,
so that something like
that warping flame might one day
scare the devil out of me.

Another Tower of Babel

Over the years, I have farmed
a cacophony of voices,
some ancestral, some speaking
through walls or mirrors,
others blabbering in tongues.

I remember neon-dyed chicks
crammed inside crude wooden cages
in Bangkok's Weekend Market.

In Khartoum
my teacher thought I was a mute,
amazed one day to hear me
gibbering to my brother,
after thinking I was autistic.

"A door opened and I went through it."
"Yes you did, and I held it."

Still, those fledglings flurried in
with their ludicrous feathers,
my mind, its own Tower of Babel,
with a strangeness I can't escape.

For My Japanese Grandfather, An Elegy

In Hawaii, my grandfather dove
into the Pacific's waves
from the well of his fishing boat,
scuba tank on his back,
running on oxygen,
as he fluttered down to spike fish
to be later sold as delicacies,
bubbling past cowrie-shell lures,
his wooden spear with a
bird bone point, lighter than air.

Did he know what was coming
or was already lost, as the low moon
pulled at blue strings of the tide,
determining fate, or luck,
before he rose again, from the ocean
like Jesus from the stations of the cross?

And on the Japanese New Year,
my mother remembers going
with him to the open market, where
vendors hawked their goods, teaching her how
to choose the freshest fish,
with the clearest bull's eyes,
no blood in the pupil's white ring.

Now, as we walk down the aisles
at an Asian supermarket,
my mother points out the ones
she finds best, brightest and plump,
scales glinting on white floes of ice,
as she taps her finger on the glass,
directing the fishmonger
to scrape off the gills, ghastly eyes
as if they'd been shocked.

Later, as we prepare to steam
them, I hold one in my hand
the way my grandfather must've done,
betting on hope, then luck,
and reaching up into the night sky,
a handful of stars, to toss like coins
into the depths of her heart,
an offering from her father's ghost
walking the planks
or a daughter's prayer
that her every wish,
could at last come true.

My Mother Is Like the Snowball Flower

It doesn't matter
if the blossoms are white, pink,
violet—they all rise to the sun.

Each flower,
a nest of tiny brass thimbles,
or expanded as baby-birds'
open beaks.

On bad nights, when I was
subsumed by fever or nightmares,
she would sit by my bed
and I would imagine
a few petals strewn apart:

the crook of her arm
with the birthmark shaped

like a three-leaf clover.

Playing Old Records in Khartoum

My parents listened to the
wistful music of the Carpenters
on the old record player
shipped from the States,

albums in cardboard sleeves
stacked up on a shelf,
in that hot, fly-swatted house
where electricity was scarce.

They sat on the rattan sofa
holding hands, eyes closed,
the corners of their mouths upturned.

What did I know of their lives
before I was born? When did their
happiness turn to pain?

Skipped memories replay in my mind,
the record's grooves blackly warped
and spinning,
but now scratched too deep.

Hawaiian Geese

> *The state bird of Hawaii is called the nene. They descended from Canadian geese a half-million years ago, not long after the island of Hawaii was formed.*

On a corner table,
a stuffed Hawaiian goose and gosling
that my mother brought home
from the Palolo Valley
where she grew up;
after her grandparents
immigrated from Okinawa.

A lonely only child, she
played house with a cardboard box,
walked a mile uphill
to get home from Sunday school.
Marrying my father,
she later raised five children.

Now, my father is dead,
my mother and I live here
in Virginia, where Canadian geese
paddle in the pond,
pecking at grass seed.
During flight they change position
to break the wind,
allowing those who follow revive.

If my mother's calm and gentle voice
is like the nene,
I am a gosling shadowing.

The stuffed mother and child nene
have indigo and white patterns,
in soft canvas cotton.
The gosling is half as tall.

While Canadian geese coast over
water and different lands,
the nene stay more on the ground,
closer to home. As if I could fly,
from each bird I have inherited a wing.

Jennie Mintz has a multicultural heritage of Jewish and Japanese descent. She was born in Singapore, and due to her father's work with the USAID, she attended international schools in Jakarta, Indonesia; Khartoum, Sudan; Bangkok, Thailand; and New Delhi, India.

She has earned a BA from George Mason University and an MA from American University and has done volunteer work with the National Alliance on Mental Illness (NAMI) and public libraries and resides in Northern Virginia.

www.ingramcontent.com/pod-product-compliance
Lightning Source LLC
LaVergne TN
LVHW041516070426
835507LV00012B/1619